Age Range: This book is suitable for readers aged 18 and above due to its mature themes and complex exploration of social issues.

Title: The Pride: People of Colors

Subtitle: Embracing Diversity and Celebrating Unity

Genre: Fiction

Themes: Diversity, Identity, Unity, Empowerment

Categories: Contemporary Fiction, Social Issues, Cultural Diversity

Chapter 1: A Colorful Beginning

In the opening chapter of "The Pride: People of Colors," readers are introduced to a vibrant and diverse community known as The Pride. Set in the bustling

city of Harmony Ville, the story unveils the lives of individuals from different ethnicities, backgrounds, and cultures. Amidst the hustle and bustle of daily life, the chapter focuses on the lives of five main characters:

Maya, a talented artist from a multicultural family; Raj, a passionate advocate for social justice; Carmen, a spirited dancer with a deep

Table of Content:

Description:

"The Pride: People of Colors" is a captivating fiction novel that delves into the lives of individuals from diverse cultural backgrounds, as they navigate their identities, confront societal challenges, and discover the power of unity. Through interconnected storylines and compelling characters, this book explores the importance of embracing diversity and celebrating the richness of different cultures. It sheds light on the struggles, triumphs, and shared experiences of people of color, highlighting the transformative impact of unity and understanding.

connection to her heritage; Liam,

an aspiring musician navigating his

identity; and Aisha,

a determined student committed

to breaking stereotypes.

As the chapter unfolds, readers witness the

challenges and triumphs these characters

face in their personal lives and within the

larger community.

From navigating cultural expectations to

confronting prejudice and discrimination,

they each begin to recognize the power

and beauty of their

unique identities.

Chapter 2: Threads of Unity

In Chapter 2 of "The Pride: People of Colors," the focus shifts towards the growing sense of unity and solidarity among The Pride. The characters find themselves crossing paths and forming deep connections, discovering shared experiences and common goals. The chapter delves Into the various ways The Pride comes together, be it through community events, cultural celebrations, or collaborative projects. They learn to appreciate and celebrate each other's traditions, languages, and customs, finding strength in their diversity.

As the bonds within The Pride strengthen, they begin to explore ways to create positive change in their community. They organize discussions, workshops, and outreach programs to raise awareness about the importance of inclusivity, acceptance, and understanding.

Chapter 3: Facing Adversity

Chapter 3 of "The Pride: People of Colors" delves into the challenges and obstacles the characters encounter on their journey towards empowerment.

The chapter explores instances of discrimination, stereotyping, and systemic inequalities that impact their lives.

Through personal narratives and shared experiences, the characters confront adversity head-on, finding the courage to speak up against injustice.

They develop resilience, determination, and a sense of purpose in their pursuit of equality and social change.

The chapter highlights the importance of self-reflection, empathy, and allyship as The Pride collectively works towards dismantling barriers and fosteringa a more inclusive society.

Chapter 4: Voices Amplified

In Chapter 4 of "The Pride: People of Colors," the characters find their voices amplified as they engage in activism and advocacy. They join forces with other like-minded individuals and organizations, amplifying their message of equality and justice. Through peaceful protests, artistic expressions, and community initiatives, The Pride raises awareness about the issues affecting people of colors.

They strive to create spaces where everyone's voices are heard, ensuring that marginalized communities receive the representation they deserve.

The chapter emphasizes the power of collective action and the strength of unity in bringing about meaningful change. The characters recognize the importance of solidarity and the impact they can make when they work together towards a common goal.

Chapter 5: Celebrating Heritage

Chapter 5 of "The Pride: People of Colors" is dedicated to celebrating the rich heritage and cultural traditions of The Pride. The characters immerse themselves in cultural festivals, culinary experiences, and artistic showcases, showcasing the beauty and diversity of their backgrounds. Through vibrant descriptions and heartfelt moments, readers are invited to embrace appreciation. The chapter highlights the significance of cultural preservation and the importance of passing down traditions to future generations.

It emphasizes the strength and beauty that comes from embracing and honoring one's roots.

The chapter highlights the significance of cultural preservation and the importance of passing down traditions to future generations. It emphasizes the strength and beauty that comes from embracing and honoring one's roots.

Chapter 6: Breaking Barriers

As the members of The Pride continue to build connections and foster understanding, they find themselves faced with the challenge of breaking down barriers that have long divided their communities.

They organize town hall meetings, community events, and cultural exchanges, creating spaces where open dialogue and shared experiences can bridge the gaps between different cultures.

In Chapter 6, we follow the journey of Maya, a young artist who uses her creativity as a means of breaking barriers.

Maya organizes an art exhibition showcasing the works of artists from diverse backgrounds.
Through their art, they challenge stereotypes, celebrate cultural heritage, and invite viewers
to engage in meaningful conversations about race, identity, and unity.
Meanwhile, Raj, a first-generation immigrant, starts a mentorship program to support young individuals from marginalized communities.
He believes that education and guidance can empower individuals to overcome obstacles and succeed in their chosen paths.

Raj's program receives overwhelming support from members of The Pride, who recognize the importance of uplifting the next generation.

Chapter 7: Finding Common Ground
In Chapter 7, The Pride takes their mission of unity and empowerment to new heights.

They organize a community festival that celebrates the diverse cultures within their neighborhood.

The festival becomes a vibrant showcase of music, dance, food, and traditions from around the world.

People of all backgrounds come together, forming connections and finding common ground through shared experiences. During the festival, Sarah, a young journalist, conducts interviews with members of The Pride and attendees to capture their stories of resilience and triumph. Through her articles, she aims to inspire others to embrace diversity and challenge prejudice.

Chapter 8: The Power of Unity

In Chapter 8, The Pride faces a significant challenge when their community becomes the target of an act of discrimination and hatred.

A local business owned by a member of

The Pride is vandalized, sending

shockwaves through the community.

Instead of succumbing to fear and despair,

The Pride rallies together, organizing

peaceful protests and advocating

for justice.

Their united front attracts the attention

of local leaders, community organizations,

and the media.

The story of The Pride's resilience and

determination spreads far and wide,

inspiring other communities to stand

up against discrimination and

embrace diversity.

Chapter 9: Voices of Change

Chapter 9 focuses on the amplification of voices within The Pride.

Through public speaking engagements, social media campaigns, and grassroots initiatives, members of The Pride raise their voices to bring about systemic change.

They advocate for policy reformof education programs promoting cultural understanding, and increased representation in positions of power.

Their efforts attract support from allies across various communities, sparking a movement for greater inclusivity and social justice. The Pride becomes a beacon of the community.

Chapter 10: Embracing the Future

In the final chapter of "The Pride: People of Colors," the members of The Pride reflect on their journey and celebrate their accomplishments. They gather for a special event where they share stories of personal growth, community transformation, and the power of unity. During this event, the community comes together to honor the achievements of The Pride and recognize the positive impact they have made.

Local leaders and representatives from different organizations express their gratitude for the Inspiration and change brought about by The Pride's efforts.

As the chapter unfolds, The Pride unveils their plans for the future.

They envision a world where diversity is celebrated, where people of all colors, backgrounds, and identities can thrive without fear of discrimination or prejudice.

They commit to continuing their work, building bridges, and fostering understanding to create a more inclusive society.

In the closing moments of the story, the members of The Pride stand united, symbolizing the strength and resilience of a community that has embraced their unique identities and come together to make a difference.

Their journey is a testament to the power of unity, the importance of embracing diversity, and the potential for positive change when people of colors join forces.

Conclusion:

"The Pride: People of Colors" is a powerful And inspiring story that explores the themes Of diversity, unity, and social change. It celebrates the strength of individual s coming Together to overcome adversity and create a More inclusive world. Through its engaging narrative and compelling Characters, the book encourages readers of all Ages to reflect on their own role in promoting

Equality and understanding.

It sparks conversations about the

Importance of embracing diversity,

breaking down barriers,

and working towards a future where

everyone is respected and valued.

With its powerful message,

"The Pride: People of Colors" is a must-must

-read for anyone seeking inspiration, hope,

and a vision for a more inclusive society.

It reminds us that by standing together and

celebrating our differences,

we can create a world where everyone has

the opportunity to thrive and be proud of

who they are.

Thanks for Reading !

Also Read:

1- The billionaire's Secretary
2-Only A Queer
3- The digital Age:
4- The Digital Revolution:
5-Avoid Depression
6- The secret keeper

Written by John Kimberly